AF243979

IN FIDELITY

COURTNEY O'BANION SMITH

Winner of the
2022 Catherine Case Lubbe Manuscript Prize
of the Poetry Society of Texas

This publication is the winner of the 2022 Catherine Case Lubbe Manuscript Contest sponsored by the Poetry Society of Texas.

Published by the Poetry Society of Texas.

This competition is an annual contest with a deadline of August 1. Complete rules and guidelines are available from poetrysocietyoftexas.org or Richard Kushmaul:

9612 Sandlewood Drive
Denton, TX 76207
704-608-9702
richardkdpa@gmail.com

FIRST EDITION

Editor: Susan Maxwell Campbell
Judge: Bruce Bond
Cover Art: *A Mermaid's Love* by Catrin Welz-Stein

ISBN: 978-0-9962311-4-5

*For Jack Bat, the nugget,
and the women, real and imagined,
who saw and showed me.*

CONTENTS

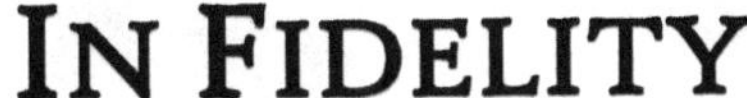

It's very difficult to keep the line between the past and the present.
Know what I mean?

Little Edie, *Grey Gardens*

DOCUMENTARIAN

She sorts inchmeal through a dusty shoebox
stuffed with frayed photographs—her mother's last
haphazard stash of odd preservations,
memories someone else might want someday.

A nonsensical collage on the floor,
she fights the urge to retouch the past since
even honest archivists can comment
accidentally with a bad angle

or overexpose for ill-gotten gains.
Her mercurial father smiles in one—
faded, light eyes still hard, checking trotlines
on a muggy night. Lines constellated

across the murky wet, hooks wait hidden
in bait seined from sloughs with her, his pupil,
in the river bottom, their school. Snapshots
of fancy chickens, a truck bed camper

turned aviary for flea market birds—
eccentric dots of canicular days'
connections now cooled in the aperture
of her flawed mind's eye. Which to toss or save

to scan into ether and for whom? She
believes the answers matter because who
ever questions monochrome's verity
despite cut and paste or who left what out?

AROUND THE FIRE

What was it like? Well, we believed

our little corner was everything

and like everywhere else

                      and always would be.

Parties every week complete

with inflatable water slides and broken,

                      plastic parting gifts.

Stretchy pants so we could super-size

patties made of a thousand animals each.

A square of yellow for a little extra,

and we always paid

                      for a little extra.

We had so much, we thought

we were starving if we didn't get

what we felt like right away.

                      Even our pets on diets.

Back then, two gas stations for every house.

Cars because of sprawl. Sprawl because of cars.

Fake tans because the sun

                      had already begun

                      to kill us. And the storms.

Too much rain over too much concrete,

tides rose to meet floodwaters. Man versus

God with all the gadgets with all the news

all the time about celebrities we

wanted to be, politicians we blamed,

> and friends we couldn't make.

I remember this one time, my mother's eyes

brimming, looking at one of her screens, soft

rustle of her neon acrylic nails

digging into the skirt of her cotton dress

patterned with huge, hot pink hibiscus

> gone now forever.

This time, she answered when I asked why

she cried. *The very last male white rhino*

in the entire world just died, she sighed,

like she was reading the last line at bedtime

> from an ancient, beloved book.

She might as well have said

> a unicorn.

She wiped her nose with a tissue, gripped her gold cross.

Now, don't litter, baby. Go throw your wrapper

> *in the trash.*

Still so many species then.

> We were convinced

> we still looked good,

at least from the shoulders up.

I shouldn't blame her. What could she have done

really? The world had already been

> lit on fire.

VAN GOGH'S *THE BEDROOM*

On the way to his psychiatrist appointment, he says there's no good place to put the bed. He says his pillows, flat sheet, and stuffed T. Rex always fall in the gap between the mattress and the wall because of the shape of his room. Maybe we could move it to the other side of the room, swap places with the dark IKEA dresser in the corner, put the bed below the blue bits of sticky tack constellated across the wall charting where his drawings used to be. But then the bed would be right next to the window, he says. A werewolf or a ghost could see him through the crack between the apple-green curtain and the window. But maybe not if we duct-taped the curtain to the wall. We're ten minutes late instead of twenty minutes early. She adds another pill. That's five now. Half his age. I stare at my phone as she scribbles. A picture of him three summers ago at the Van Gogh exhibit sitting in the life-sized, slanted replica of the artist's bedroom at Arles. A room from a painting with the painter's paintings hanging above the bed. He grins in the cane-bottom chair closest to me. So much butter yellow like his hair. So much French blue like his eyes. The diorama is mostly true, but the green-framed window next to the bed behind him sits wide open. The doctor asks if I've made my own appointment yet. My son draws another picture.

> *keep the window closed—*
> *superheroes' portraits watch,*
> *safer than landscapes*

THE VIEWING

WHITE OAK, Miocene Epoch
Houston Museum of Natural Science

It took twenty million years to get here:
shiny cross-section of petrified white oak—
disk displayed as lighted evidence of the death
of my grandfather more than thirty years ago.

The pale wood turned smooth black stone of filigreed rings,
spiderweb-thin grooves that filtered oxygen for generations
bisected by a tube of white *where ground water*
brought in oxygen and bleached away the dark cellulose
present in the mineralized wood: a trachea
whose blackened lobes inhaled smoke instead of air.

My father's father rolled cigarettes
in a green tin lawn chair on his front porch,
knees crossed in polyester khakis. King Edward VII
watched over the loose molasses-smelling tobacco
from the underside of the lid-flap
of the yellow cardboard cigar box.
The pink tip of Grandpa's tongue
dampened the edge of the thin white paper translucent.
Yellowed, thick fingers and fingernails
delicately picked off flecks of tobacco as he spat.
The strike, the flair, the sharp sulfur odor
commingled with the sweet exhalation of white smoke
drifting between chipped white columns.

I was seven but not the youngest
when the family gathered inside his white wooden house.
Grandma's wails overtook the quieter
crying of his grown children that first woke me.
I was led in to see the shell he had left of himself.
Brown and yellow striped curtains.
Soft white glow of a lacy lampshade.

My little brain couldn't contain
the entire scene. I looked for it,
but his tongue was lost
in the blackness of his gaping mouth.

Even at seven, I was offended by
the tasteful artifice of the dead:
Mouth closed. Skin pinkened
for display. Face swollen
behind pointless square glasses over
sunken eyelids. Fingers and nails
now caked in flesh-toned makeup
folded gently at the waist in affected repose.

Standing in the museum's darkened room
filled with roundish slabs lit by spotlights,
I can see some beauty in it now.
They lived once and continue to matter,
although in an altered state—
imposed memories, a satisfying obsequy
for those left behind—
even if only for a moment,
to viewers filing past one at a time.

TIME ENOUGH AT LAST

Her daddy's dusty shoebox of broken
wrist watches still sits untouched on a shelf—
someone else's wasted time, abandoned
distractions for tinkering collected
from garage sales since well before he passed
ten years ago. Bodies remain buried

beneath the twisted wreckage of wrist bands,
but some still whir or eke out a dragging,
infinitesimal pulse, now almost
imperceptible. Nevertheless, her
mama won't throw his box away even
after the last ticks its last—its second

hand stopped between two marks on its round face.
Meanwhile, her mama's museum-worthy
display of cheap timepieces hangs arranged
in the living room. Each pendulum swings
at its own pace counting down the seconds
she has then has no more—celestial

score to which she reads the world away.
Her mama claims she can't know exactly
how much time until whatever's coming
comes. Besides, faith set in such collections
born of fear of the inevitable
is unreliable. So, her daughter

keeps only a single clock in each room
at any time; all other time-telling
apparatus must be checked at the door.
Every lone clock is accurately set
so she knows what to do when. Alarm bells
dictate life's business from sleep to safe sleep.

She wants temporal precision because,
though time can't be altogether banished,
it can at least be managed. Otherwise,
how would she assess her existence, know
no matter where or when she is, she is
or when there will be time enough at last?

MONO NO AWARE

*Japanese term for the awareness of impermanence, a
transient wistfulness as well as a deeper, gentle sadness
about this state being the reality of life*

After each betrayal, she bought herself
flowers, but only the ones on clearance—
bunches in clear cellophane rotting in buckets
hidden but discoverable
by those who knew where to look
in the grocery store's floral department.
Every time she imagined the other women,
she bought bunches of mums
shedding purple tear-shaped petals when jostled,
wilted roses, rainbow-hued buds too open and bruised,
or limp poms, heads downcast with all they'd seen.
Pretty soon, each room had its own bargain bouquet
pieced together with blooms on their way out—
just enough beauty left in them
to prove that, for a moment,
something beautiful had existed
even if her dream couldn't possibly last.

Up Early

Blind-broken, Texas sun already hot,
my father'd stand in my doorway, stained cap
in hand, a sweaty alarm clock set on
telling me how half the day's gone by nine.
Smelling of cut grass or manure, he loved
telling me, no matter how old I was,
how I never got up early enough.
He knew, out of necessity, the day's
potential wakes before the light begins.
Now, as I leave in the quiet dark to beat
rush hour, my sons sleep just as ignorant
as I was. What other wisdom of his
will I find as the years without him
accumulate one sunrise at a time?

THE DEPUTY AND HIS PARTNER

paddled up our driveway, our personal
Noahs in yellow rain slickers and straw Stetsons,
because only our porch light was on.
Bags of dirt barricaded the door.

Do you need evacuation? he yelled
through the window over thunder
and rushing water. I worried he'd wake
the boys from their sodden slumber.

To where? The search light's beam illuminated
only the drops that passed through,
bounced off dark windows of the other houses,
haunted ships on the new sea of our street.

Shelter. I need to know now.
We're not coming back.

He was telling the truth.
But the boys sleep so deeply when it rains.

They floated off past the stop sign,
and the rain kept falling.

PLUNDER

The Bidai Indians still seemed to live there
in the slant of autumnal light through oak limbs
and the rush and gurgle of murky water
where one-hundred-pound yellow cat and alligator gar
lurked along the riverbed. Snapping turtles' heads
broke the surface and slipped silently under again—
their red stripes an ancient warning.

After a gully-washer, the river always called
the prodigal water back eventually
leaving sloughs filled with careless crawfish
and minnows we'd sein
for trotline bait once the roads
became passable. We'd all head
to Horseshoe Bend and comb the latest layer
stripped clean for new riches
from the land's long-gone residents.

But there will be no more shouts
when the camouflage of dead oak leaves
gives way to arrowheads and spear points,
our plunder. Knowing it would one day happen,
my family mounted each treasure
behind glass, the practical appropriated
as ornament and nostalgia for a people
we pretended we were related to.

The greedy Navasota River has finally claimed
that patch of earth—the highest point now
a tiny island for lounging turtles until the next big rain.

APOLOGY WITH GRATITUDE

Save me from these evil deeds before I get them done.
Fiona Apple, "Criminal"

You bask in the blinding bomb
of a sun that warms your wind-chilled skin
while you wait in line to cast your vote
to make yourself feel a certain way
at the beginning of the end.

You look through your narrow lens of bias
dizzily searching for the thing
you think is truth on the ballot screen.
There's no chance for redemption
when you know and you know you know,
and you go despite what you could do differently:

I'm sorry, you say to the future
as you lift a plastic bag of diet sodas
into the back of your hybrid automobile.

I'm sorry, you say to the future
as you carry the blue recycle bin to the curb.

I'm sorry, as you run the sprinklers,
empty the dishwasher, burn the burgers,
drag your finger over strangers' feeds.

I'm sorry, as you scramble
yolk and albumen, the culmination of multitudes
evolved from feathered dinosaurs
to end up as your breakfast.

I can't say we didn't know, you say
stirring the cage-free progeny
as it fries in butter in your Teflon pan.

We keep pretending, you say,
and believing. You take another bite
of the fragile, broken present.

MIRROR, MIRROR

These chin hairs were passed down to me
by my mother, my grandmothers,
their mothers, and all the scary old crones
who live in candy cabins and poison or eat
the young and beautiful in fairy tales
told before bed. Dark strands
twisted as thornbushes grow while I sleep,
await diurnal discovery in my mirror
magicked with magnified light
to better tell the brutal truth.
Countless potions, princes' kisses,
and consultations with medical magicians
could never break the spell
of my mammalian inheritance.
Some strands grow back white now,
but, at times, I don't envy smooth, taut skin—
youth's compensation for inexperience.
There are days I might even love
the wise, wrinkled, and bewhiskered "witch"
they say I'm turning into. Each morning,
I recognize—by a hair's breadth more—
how often the villainess was written off,
just how much she was misunderstood.

TWEEZING

When my 79-year-old mother visits,
she asks me to weed the wild field
of her face. Her long lashes
my sons and I inherited lace closed
as she waits trusting as a baby.
I don't bother with her hirsute
upper lip or thin thatch of brows.
Involuntary jerk with each quick yank,
her tilted chin is an invitation
to inflict pain only a daughter
can accept, a readiness to suffer
only a mother can offer.

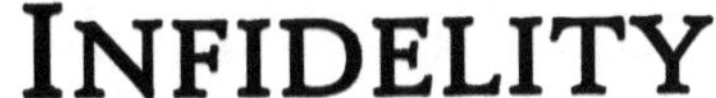 INFIDELITY

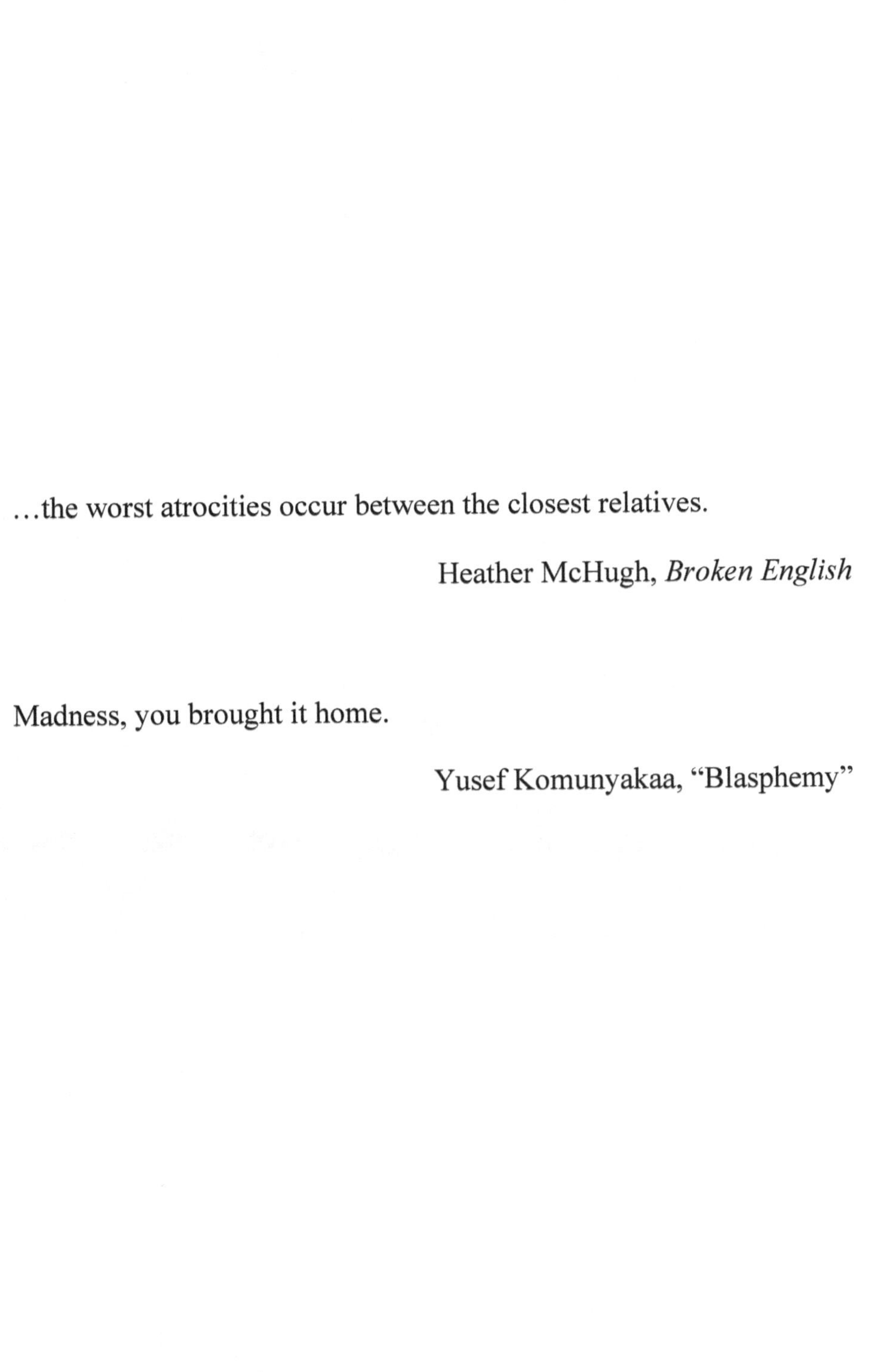

…the worst atrocities occur between the closest relatives.

Heather McHugh, *Broken English*

Madness, you brought it home.

Yusef Komunyakaa, "Blasphemy"

Mama Lydie's Percy

Texas, 1915

In the evening, my shoulders are wings
of shadow. The groove in the trunk
where my back fits
is damn near worn smooth.

Hickory tree ain't far enough
from the house. I still hear
the children yell Daddy
or Mama Lydie call my name
that sounds like mercy
coming out her mouth.

Surprised the gun fit
in these hands, hard
from woodwork and cotton bolls.

Nestled against my tree,
I sat rock still just before.
Her yelling my name
and my boy yelling Daddy—
top half of them floating
over cotton plants as they ran
toward me arms wide
like at a homecoming.

My whittling takes privacy.
They don't understand that
even now that I'm gone.

The floor of heaven is covered
with wood shavings. My family's love sits
white and soft in cracked pods
that bloody fingers till they're numb.

Mama Lydie's Reply

I came down like water
from the angel slaughter,
loose and glum, unable to fit
inside my own skin anymore,
too big with what I'd seen.

Percy was sneaky
with his writings and doings,
slick and unfettered without
a normal man's conscience.
Blue and me sailed over the cotton,

flew despite our feet
as the sun set, but not even our voices
could push through the breeze
in his favorite tree or his resolve,
not as fast as the bullet sliced his brain

and stuck forever in the trunk.
Percy's notes of Hell's train depot
just down the road and poisoned water
in the cisterns brought on
by the government or witches' curses

somehow whooshed off his pages
into people's hearts despite my silence
or his sons' shame. Distrust followed him
everywhere—even home.
Blue was too close to the moment

of his daddy's shadow's separation.
His release may one day whisper
down gentle and slow like the rain
of leaves after the thunder
of that single shot. But Percy's relief

so swiftly delivered
now rests on my shoulders
where his sweaty gibberish
used to live. It is more full of light
and barely makes a sound.

I can still hear it though,
sweeter than seraphim's laughter
and Blue's baby brother's breath.
I pray Blue receives it in his dreams, but
please God, may it not come out his hands.

PRAYERS OVER DIRTY DISHES

1934

Pleased to see a dead snake belly-up
in the road, Ruthlyn mentions rain
to Blue. Silently thanking God for little things,
Ruthlyn dips her hands in greasy dishwater.

She prays for the soap to sud,
the grasshoppers to pass over the garden,
the marks not to show.
She knows better than to ask
Blue to stop. He is a force
beyond insects and weather.

Ruthlyn, whose flour-sack dresses are all full
for expectation, pushes loose strands
of her dark hair behind her left ear
straining for any sign of rain.

She listens hard from the kitchen.
Hands searching in gray water,
she cocks her head, eavesdrops on footfalls,
watches for clouds, and keeps praying
for some spare grace or mercy.

HOUSE DANCE

1935

As if to say stepping is high time,
Beau's flames of hair
flounce as he moves.
He accepts a mason jar
of white lightning
to dull the moon's glow
in his eyes. His hot breath
fizzles in a blonde's ear.
Her name is Lucy,
but he doesn't ask.

Dance with me?
Come on, darlin'.
What you got to lose?

But it's some other broad
who struggles after Beau's wingtips
as he floats across the floor
on the kind of whispered promises
he never keeps.

Lucy pouts in the corner,
and her regular guy
puts his arm around her.
Lucy's lip shrivels
as her shoulders throw him off.

Beau winks at the other man
and laughs at what he knows
a jilted lady can set in motion.

Later, Beau laughs against his pickup
shining in the moonlight
retelling the story through a split lip.

His hair flares like a campfire
at an all-night fish fry. He leans on Lucy
under his arm, another detail
he's already beginning to forget.

THE WATERING HOLE

Trying to impress her, Beau says,
*Fish smell through their skin, so
smelling is like tasting to 'em.*
He says, *Fish don't remember
hardly nothing. Guess they're
lucky that way.* She hides

her face under her floppy hat
and watches his cork
as it bobs, then disappears.
Beau swings the cane
and snags a bass. He whistles
his approval of its size
as it gleams dripping at the end
of his line. She watches the bass
drown in air as love
leaps between them.

A keeper, he says.

Ruthlyn squints at the fish
as Beau lowers it to the ground.

The fish curls its back and raises
its tail, slower each time.
Red clay dust gums
the fish's pearlescent belly
swollen with eggs.

Ruthlyn draws a finger along
its black stripe and wonders
what she tastes like to it.
Careful of its spiny back fin,
she removes the hook from its jaw
despite its slippery body
or jerks of panic at her alien touch.

Beau's grin wanes as she puts the fish
back where it belongs.

HER GIFT

She doubts that she'll ever wear
the lemon-drop dream,
but it doesn't much matter to her.

Beau scratches the stubble of his cleft chin.
I saw it, baby, and I thought
well now, there's something
as pretty as my honey—
something that rivals
the morning like my baby.

Ruthlyn eyes the hat
in the round box. The scentless mess
of yolk-colored gossamer roses
stitched at the crimp above the brow
holds the brim to a band of satin sunlight.
Its yellow impracticality pleases her.

Now we just got to get you
to a place to wear it, you reckon?

Ruthlyn covers a smile
as the tissue paper fusses with the breeze.
Where could they possibly go?

She loves the hat
maybe more than him,
her one gift and only possession.

FISHING ON THE FLOOR

She hit the floor knees first.
The tomato stake landed
hollowly beside her. The screen door settled
on the second bounce as Blue stomped
down the front porch steps under
the dim yellow of a bare light bulb.

Green yaupon as thick as a man's thumb
hacked to a point at one end,
the stake was meant to save the heavy fruit
from ants and the vine from splitting—
its branches curving downward
with the ripe weight and sticky
summer heat. She learned a long time ago
not to whimper. Pain
sometimes liked a voice,
but he never did.

In the kitchen, jars of skinless,
red globes floating in juice
rattled on the shelves
to the rhythm of Blue's self-righteous exit
into the humid dark.
Her silent mouth opened and closed
as she tried to get her breath
like that bass drowning in fear
on the stock tank's red-dirt bank.

Ruthlyn pulled her knees to her chest
and dreamed of fishing with another man.

LUCKY

The dice bounce and jig in the lantern light
to the sound of the gulps and cheers
of men too poor to be betting the hard way.

Beau's up a Hamilton and worth his shine.
His hair flames above a stone-cold smirk.
It don't take much to break a man
these days, but Beau's betting anyway.
Blue's gut dooms his overalls,
swings low near the saddle blanket
as he hovers over a few sweaty bucks
in front of him. Whiskey-soaked voices holler.

com'on baby
seven seven
seven eleven com'on
wooooo-eeeeee
roll them dice Beau

Blue's hard eyes stare at the brother
who loves his wife,
whose grin makes Lady Luck swoon.

roll 'em agin Beau
roll them dice boy
roll them dice

Moonshine blurs Beau's gaze
as each crumpled bill finds its way
to his end of the blanket.
Blue grunts softly to his feet,
spits his tobacco, swigs his jug,
lurks off into the dark woods
to hide and wait.

WHERE IT DON'T SHOW

Didn't pull the trigger but might as well have.
My mama said your mama was the one that done it—
made your daddy nuts.
You gonna cry now, fatso?
Gonna cry 'cause it's true I bet, crybaby!
Cry why don't you, you little pissant runt.
Butterball with scrawny grasshopper legs.
Nah, more like a toad,
>*ugly face*
>>*and big ol' gut.*

The boy pulls up Blue's shirt,
>exposes a flabby belly
>as white as the schoolhouse
>Blue's backed against.
The others laugh their approval.

Jab of a pointy finger.
>*Can you hop, toad-boy?*

Jab and Blue's body jerks, laughter.
>*Bet you're mama's crazy little baby, ain't ya toady.*

Jab-jerk.
>*Go home to your mama, frog-face.*

The bruises form soon, just under flannel
buttoned until bedtime.

What's that, Blue? Beau asks with a lisp
>born from no front teeth.

Don't you tell Mama, hear?
You tell Mama and you'll pay.
I swear to God, Beau.

Don't swear to God, Blue.
I won't tell nobody.
Promise.
          Does it hurt?

What you think?
Nothing hurts me.
          But I'll hurt you where it don't show
if you don't keep your mouth shut.

Beau rolls over and pretends
to be brave enough to sleep.

DAY OF REST

I.

I can tell you hatred of your daddy has a flavor—
rancid like spoiled fish and tough
in the mouth like burnt fried okra.

While Mama and Beau was getting right with Jesus,
it happened—maybe because
I was never invited.

Daddy's hair slicked back with pomade,
face flushed but not from shame,
madness crowed and strutted
at the head of our dinner table.

We'd say grace like an unwritten letter:

> *Dear Heavenly Father,*
>
> *Thank You for Your bounty*
> *and protection from evil.*
>
> *In Jesus' name we pray,*
>
> *Amen.*

and turn our plates over.

II.

Good God, she loved Sundays.
Giddy from communion,
she floated around the house
from laundry to dishes,
holy the rest of the day,
humming her hymns and concentrating
on her tasks like a girl that plays
mostly by herself.

While she worked, I took Beau to the woods
where I taught him the pecking order.

WELL, BEAU NEVER DID SHY AWAY

from liquor or a fight.

You know how he was.
Blue wasn't much different
and he was biding his time
waiting for him
that night in those woods.

You know their daddy was crazy.
Sure, y'all remember Percy.
Maybe Blue took after his daddy.
Anyway, Blue was waiting for Beau
like I said. Well,
Blue had a tire-iron.
Ambushed Beau after losing craps,
his own damn brother now,
and worked him over good
like a piece of tough meat
before you fry it. I hear
Beau egged him on.
Guess a man
can only take so much.

You know how Beau is, too.
Say anything to get you riled.
Now Beau's up in the state hospital.
There ain't no other place for him really.
No wife or mama to take care of him.
Can't talk worth a damn.
Just slobbers all the time,
slack-jawed and practically toothless.
Only one eye and the opposite ear.
I seen him firsthand.

You know, his face looks like
it's sewed together

from all them damn stitches.
Reminds me of that monster
from that picture show.
Whatsit called?
That's right. Frankenstein.
Bald spots all over his head,
bits of scalp knocked off.
Head caved in here and here.
Plumb pathetic.

You know, I heard Blue beat that woman
of his, pretty regular too,
and I believe it. That man's meaner
than a damn mama sow.
There ain't no accounting
for that kind of mean,
and over a little bit of money.
It don't make no sense.

You know, that's one hell of a way
to treat your own damn family.

Trinity: A Confession

They will probably kill me for killing you.

You filled the doorway with your breath's heat,
your body's weight, your fists
like boulders rolled away from tombs,
blood all over your face.
No humility. You filled the room
with what you did to him
and then you did it to me.

So exhausted from so much invention,
secret movements,
tricks of light and shadow—
I loaded the gun slowly.

Your throaty snores from the bedroom
were the final music flooding over
my bruised face like a baptism,
like permission:
the score to my own short-lived exodus.
I even heard an angel say,

Do it.

So I sent you to Heaven.
More than you deserve.

> *Operator? Get me the Sheriff.*
> *Hello, Walter? Yes.*
> *Well, in a manner of speaking.*
> *You need to come get me.*
> *I shot Blue in the head*
> *while he was sleeping.*

My boys got there first.
I was in the rocking chair on the front porch

humming your missing music,
rocking to its rhythm
and knitting booties
for the one that's on the way.
Maybe the sister they always wanted.
Probably also their cousin.

Practically grown, they didn't yell or curse me.
They were pretty polite about it all really.
I rejected the sheriff's bloodshot eyes.
He's used to hobos and moonshine,
and I gave him more exciting business
in one night than he's had all year—
a story he'll tell in this town
six ways to Sunday.
You'll be absolved by it,
I'm sure.

You never did stop giving, did you?
Or taking away. It was high time
I returned the favor.

FIDELITY

A Mermaid's Love

After the image by Catrin Welz-Stein

My scales might as well have been a shimmering dress—
my fins, a bustle what with his top hat and sky-colored
coat of mismatched plumes sewn up the back, our chaste,
Victorian courtship. Magical. I confess I believed
he could fly. The first lie. The somber bird atop his hat,
silent accomplice, knew me for what I was, though. No,
no angel, but close enough. Like me, you probably thought
such a gentleman would hold my hand gently as I hovered
too close. His hands were soft, but I assure you,
his grip was firm despite his curved pinkie.
I might have seen his feathers were fake,
ridiculously large, that I was the only one of the three truly floating,
but they knew how I longed for sun and air
so they let me fool myself. While he posed,
my modest smile and downcast eyes belied my hair
floating like dark smoke, my unseemly tale—
the very thing that made me glide as if water were sky.
Quickened by my imagination, his pretend wings
seemed to flutter, suggested soaring. Something
jangled in his pocket. Caught. He wanted me
to save him from drowning, to buoy him up to the trees, up
to the heights we all longed for. Yes, I wanted to
too. Man, bird, me looking away, we all clung
to our guilty, disparate dreams of flight.

Keep Your Secrets

After the image by Catrin Welz-Stein

Did you sing? Or was your rusty throat too sore
from crying to say a thing? As he sat balanced
sidesaddle on your bare, feathered back so blue
it shines black, Lady Barn Swallow, were you
a willing accomplice? Did you carry him away
from that glowing prison after he stowed his secrets,
or did you deliver him to retrieve the pathetic betrayals
glowing within? Is the moon his safe or his escape?
Doesn't he know that birds make better messengers
than mounts? Why didn't you tell him that the confidences
carried in fidelity are burdens enough? Covert courier,
did he think I wouldn't see? Couldn't you see
with your wild side-eye the keyhole goes right through
to the other side? That his Lilliputian key,
although bigger than he, was too small after all?
What does he have on you, co-conspirator,
to take such a risky night flight? Gliding
between pinpricks of starlight, do you ever
make a wish, too, Lady Swallow? I need to know.
His top hat. Is it magic? Tell me;
what's that tiny, stiff man's cleverest trick?

To be best marveled in darkest night,
He hides obscene secrets in plain sight.

MAN IN TREE

After the image by Catrin Welz-Stein

Sometimes, he dons his hat and climbs a tree
believing I can't see up so high. The black bird
waits atop the branches to fly him there
whenever he wants, to remind him of his power
to choose me, another, others. He looks,
shoulders set same as always, hands
hidden in his long brown coat's pockets.
Is his expression one of longing or loathing?
The moon waxes. To hide what happened
or disappear once all is revealed? No one can see
his face, not me, not the bird, not himself.
No one but the moon. The surface of his secrets
illuminates his faceless self standing
in a tree, remembering what he's done,
what he could do again if he wishes,
under the stars, other suns of places
and futures we can only imagine.

FIRE MAID

After the image by Colette Calascione

Corseted in this orange-scaled mermaid suit,
like I weather your ravaging gaze,
I'm prepared for when Hokusai's *Great Wave*
will wash over this red-curtained stage
and the sinking ship of this red chaise.
Besides, my lounging grin shows I'm ready
for anything. You think I don't know this game?
The bubbles of my detective's pipe float
up past my tricorn hat; my hand behind
my head makes a fist as my fingers cross
behind my back. Don't you see? To swim, I
never needed my hands. My unpatched eye
gazes right back the way, I imagine,
the others must still lust after you too.

MESSENGER

After the image by Maggie Taylor

You lit the house on the prairie of our partnership
on fire with a story's beginning—an egg
that hatched yet another tired tale of his treachery.

That partially revealed secret was enough tinder
to light an inferno fueled by trust, formerly
the grease and glue for our love's long voyage.

Sparrows are dinosaurs. Not long-lost cousins
or distant descendants. Flying lizards.
I was once a fish with scales too.

That egg, odd blue oval on a note
crinkled in your claws, created destruction
barely visible to anyone not looking

for blazing smoke on the horizon. The tawny stripes
burning across your puffed chest immolated
the holy presence we once called a marriage—

now ashes blown across a parched plain of dust.
I long for the houseless sea, home I traded for air—
that element fundamental for life and flame.

PORTRAIT OF A HEART

After the image by Christian Schloe

I see everything through a scrim
of smoke, my dark lens. Air necessary
for fire and the smell of my burning flesh,
of the bright orange hole in my chest,
keeps my heart beating, smoldering.
I'm the fuel. His secret, the spark.
Everywhere, I see all the things he says
aren't there, brightened and dimmed
by my desire for his desire
to return to me. Like magic,
I keep my lace dress white.
Lungs full. Legs under me.
Store the ashes in my eyes
to stymie his lies by omission.
Hide my guilt at his betrayal.
Calm porcelain face, flushed cheeks,
pale forehead and dark hair—his Victorian
portrait of a lady. I do not know
how long a heart can smolder, only
how long since he set it ablaze.
My pinned braids stay tight, prim,
soot scented as the red flames' smoke
smudges the faded white flowers
on the blue-gray wallpaper of our bedroom—
nothing like the deep sea of my true home—
feeble attempt to pacify me. This flaming
heart destroys whatever home we make,
burns from the inside wherever I am.
Cunning ploy how we blame each other,
how he loves me yet can't stay true.
Accursed miracle of respiration,
the golden brooch below my bosom
rises and falls—another gift for show.
No one would ever believe

I once breathed water.
Sometimes, even I forget.

POET'S HOUSE

After the image by Maggie Taylor

He shipwrecked our house on his desolate prairie
so far from my sea. Are those black shriveled roots
or cracks in the dry dirt beneath its foundation?
So much dust! The only blue, besides my mood,
darkens the sky above our frontier. At twilight,
it most matches colors found only at the depth
of my original domain from where he believes
I rescued him. To purge a private provocation
where else but paper? Poemed parchments,
yellowing and scribbled, float away,
well past sunset, spiral up one after another, but
some sorrow stays. They escape, though,
not from windows or the red brick chimney,
not even the front door of robin's egg blue,
but from the side of the house—every one
born of a language for anguish
and dreams of being held and letting go.
Up they fly to become pinpoints of light
he assures me are not moon jellyfish
but constellations that we may steer by yet.

Unlock

After an image by Christian Schloe

Brave boy locked

in faded blue lifts

a key to

a black hole

in his chest. His treasure is

a man in the dark.

She Likes the Night

After the image by Christian Schloe

Gentle moth, fellow betrayed, even in the low illumination,

    I can see you are all wings.

        Feathered too yet far better than the birds

           I should never have trusted.

Your dusty forewings and hindwings lie flat,

    then fold like hands, brown yet iridescent

        beneath the crescent moon and cast of stars

           adorning my billowing smoke of hair.

What does your fleeting visit forecast,

    dark creature? A typhoon of jealousy?

    What real love looks like?

        Perched upon my finger,

your wings beat just enough breeze to blow

    my black hair back, to waft the citrus scent

        of our failing orchard on the horizon.

        You fan your somber brilliance

open and closed, soft as my decision

not to decide whether he should stay,

slow as the charred chamber doors of my heart

still hot inside my ribcage

encased in ghostly lace.

NOCTURNE

After the image by Christian Schloe

Raven for a friend,
what kind of monster am I?
The woman in red
was only the beginning.

Better to kill the wolf, as the story goes,
than tell the truth of our tryst.
So the moon may be my prisoner,
but I'm the one who's trapped

by those I refuse to disclose.
It's so exhausting being a beast
camouflaged in gentleman's clothes
just to survive. My bad omen of a pet

stares at the back of my shaggy head
from the perch of my elbow,
never lets me forget he saw it all,
he's still watching. My ears perk

as the moon whispers my secrets
between the birdcage's thin bars.
I didn't eat the boy who lied
one too many times.

I am the scared little boy,
and the man in the moon
is my most delicious deception
devoured again and again.

I'd swallow those soft stars instead
if I could only reach them—each one
another of my lady's wishes floating away
into the deep infidelity of the night sky.

THE POET

After an image by Christian Schloe

My paws become hands and the moon wanes
Because I write: Honesty is the sky
Ripped open. This howl's no longer
A siren song: not a hair-raising call

To the others whose replies
Exiled me to this forest.
The more I tell myself:
The more I see the beast in me:

The more a man I become.
I never wanted to be a wolf:
Prowling hunter baiting willing women:
Validation for the predator

I thought a man should be.
Seated at this walnut table
In my blue brass-buttoned coat,
I blot ink as words form on mottled paper:

I use this white wing feather
To tell the tales of my betrayals:
Remind myself the fear
Of pain is more painful than the pain

Itself: Deceit begets beasts:
It hurts to grow up.
Feeling for feathers, my lady
Ran her fingers through my fur;

Discovered she preferred it.
I put myself in these woods.
Mouth to the sky, my throat exposed,
Lips soft, I sing our sorrow:

Write my way out:
Arrive at an understanding:
My lady's not my muse. She's the poet
I only pretended to be.

DARWIN'S DIARY

After an image by Christian Schloe

Morpho for a monocle,
I can finally see the truth:
Blue has always been
My favorite color:
Sea of my lady's home,
The beguiling sky.
Birds still bother me;
Observe this jay on my shoulder.
But it's *Lepidoptera* who liberate,
Obliterate the obsessions
Of my once boyish mind.
It's detailed work to change:
Evolution of a life:
Catalog disrepair with a repurposed
Wing or tail feather: shiny, angled,
Seaweed-colored, shed (or plucked)
Asset retooled for revelation.
Birds deceive and tease
With the supposititious ease
Of flight, but these butterflies
Know better: Flittering graces.
Scratch paper with the nib:
My chrysalis cracks open
Along golden seams:
I journal metamorphosis:
Imago of what
We'll see.

THE COLLECTOR

After an image by Maggie Taylor

I catalog them—all the ways
he tries to make things up to me.
What is love if not cyclical?
Parts remixed in unavoidable phases
float about me. Kaleidoscopic wings
of fire-tipped yellows and watery blues

color me and this faded landscape enough.
His delicate prayers and myriad promises
his soft lips blew to me bob and weave
shiny green ribbons through random buttons
of my brown, corseted dress, my still pale fingers.
What must my expression be? Magnanimous?

No bird's nest in the bitter branches
of the dead tree behind me anymore.
Anyway, I prefer the dusted brilliance
of the blue morpho who sips ripe fruit,
who was named after Aphrodite
born from the sea like me.

No killing jar, pins, or glass boxes.
I capture them in ink in my book,
list the names they share with birds
and seafarers—sweet swallowtails,
skippers, and admirals of the air—
to chart my life and our love.

Resurrected from chrysalides,
what beauty now,
what hope in new things,
even if all tomorrows must also be
knitted together through pain.

RAINBOW VIEW

After the image by Catrin Welz-Stein

Some light is required.
Some water, some dirt
to make air's vibrant palette visible.
You kept your top hat but transformed
your coattails into fins and speckled scales.

Mine's concealed in a flared seaweed skirt—
hideaway for fiery fish lured
by my loose, dark locks shining
in the prodigal sun. We keep each other
afloat in my sea's allure, which you finally fathom.

We face our refracted future
formed from shared and confessed failures
in reapportioned awe. We now know only revelation,
the alchemy of light and our pasts,
made this multifaceted resurrection possible.

We are more one, more known—
some of me you and you me.
We will keep turning to face tomorrow's storms,
await those faint, distant rainbows
that can only come after together.

Notes & Acknowledgements

Versions of these poems first appeared in the following publications. Thank you to all the editors, readers, and volunteers for their hard work and support.

Barren Magazine: "The Deputy and His Partner"

Chaos Dive Reunion: "A Mermaid's Love," and "Poet's House"

Houston Poetry Fest 2019 Anthology: "Time Enough at Last"

Ocotillo Review: "Documentarian"

The Poetry Society of Texas Student Award Winners 2003: "Mama Lydie's Percy" originally appeared under the title "Mama Lydie's Pervey"

Relief: "The Viewing"

Synkroniciti: "Apology with Gratitude"

Syntax and Salt: "Around the Fire"

Texas Poetry Calendar 2020: "Plunder"

Vamp Cat Magazine: "Up Early" and "*mono no aware*"

"Time Enough at Last" refers to the *Twilight Zone* episode of the same name (1959).

The first two lines of "Mama Lydie's Reply" are influenced by the lyric "I came down like water / for the age of solar" from the song "The Ballad of Maxwell Demon" by Shudder to Think as encountered in the film *Velvet Goldmine* (1998).

The phrase "rival the morning" from "Her Gift" comes from a compliment August McCray pays Lorena "Lorie" Wood in *Lonesome Dove*, the miniseries adapted from the novel of the same name by Larry McMurtry that aired on CBS in 1989.

The ekphrastic poems in the section titled Fidelity are based on various pieces of contemporary surrealist art by Catrin Welz-Stein, Colette Calascione, Maggie Taylor, and Christian Schloe. Each poem shares the title with the piece of art that inspired it, and the respective artist is credited in each poem's epigraph. I would like to express my deepest gratitude to each artist for her unique vision and unending inspiration.

ABOUT THE AUTHOR

Courtney O'Banion Smith has a Master of Fine Arts in Creative Writing-Poetry from Texas State University-San Marcos, and she is pursuing a Master of Arts in Theopoetics and Writing at Bethany Theological Seminary. A Pushcart Prize nominee, her work has appeared in various publications including *Relief*, *Barren Magazine*, and *The Ocotillo Review*. She currently lives in Houston where she and her husband care for two feral boys and one neurotic dog. Find her online at www.cobanionsmith.com and @cobanionsmith.